Hummingbirds

Quinn M. Arnold

CREATIVE EDUCATION • CREATIVE PAPERBACKS

seedlings

Published by Creative Education and Creative Paperbacks
P.O. Box 227, Mankato, Minnesota 56002
Creative Education and Creative Paperbacks
are imprints of The Creative Company
www.thecreativecompany.us

Design by Ellen Huber; production by Joe Kahnke
Art direction by Rita Marshall
Printed in the United States of America

Photographs by Alamy (Danita Delimont, Dipak Pankhania),
Corbis (Thomas Kitchin & Victoria Hurst/Wave), Dreamstime
(Nick Biebach, Steve Byland, Kojihirano, Kelly Nelson,
Raymond Pauly, Pimmimemom, Dewald Reiners, James Vallee),
Getty Images (Susan Gary, Visuals Unlimited, Inc./Adam
Jones), iStockphoto (Pattie Calfy, Grafissimo, Shelly Perry),
Shutterstock (Dec Hogan, KellyNelson), SuperStock (Minden
Pictures)

Library of Congress Cataloging-in-Publication Data
Arnold, Quinn M.
Hummingbirds / Quinn M. Arnold.
p. cm. — (Seedlings)
Includes bibliographical references and index.
Summary: A kindergarten-level introduction to hummingbirds,
covering their growth process, behaviors, the places they call
home, and such defining features as their long beaks.
ISBN 978-1-60818-737-9 (hardcover)
ISBN 978-1-62832-333-7 (pbk)
ISBN 978-1-56660-772-8 (eBook)
1. Hummingbirds—Juvenile literature.
QL696.A558 A76 2016
598.7/64—dc23   2015041983
CCSS: RI.K.1, 2, 3, 4, 5, 6, 7;
RI.1.1, 2, 3, 4, 5, 6, 7; RF.K.1, 3; RF.1.1

First Edition HC 9 8 7 6 5 4 3 2 1
First Edition PBK 9 8 7 6 5 4 3 2 1

TABLE OF CONTENTS

Hello, hummingbirds!

There are hundreds
of hummingbirds.

They are some
of the smallest
birds in the
Americas.

Hummingbirds can be many bold colors.

Their fast
wings make
a humming
sound.

Hummingbirds cannot smell. But they have big eyes. They can see all around.

They
look for
flowers.

Hungry hummingbirds eat nectar.

They use their long, curved beaks.

They eat small bugs, too.

A baby hummingbird comes out of an egg. It stays in the nest. Its mother feeds it at first. Soon it can fly.

Hummingbirds hover. They fly up, down, and all around.

They look for food.

17

Goodbye, hummingbirds!

Picture a Hummingbird

wings

eye

feathers

tail

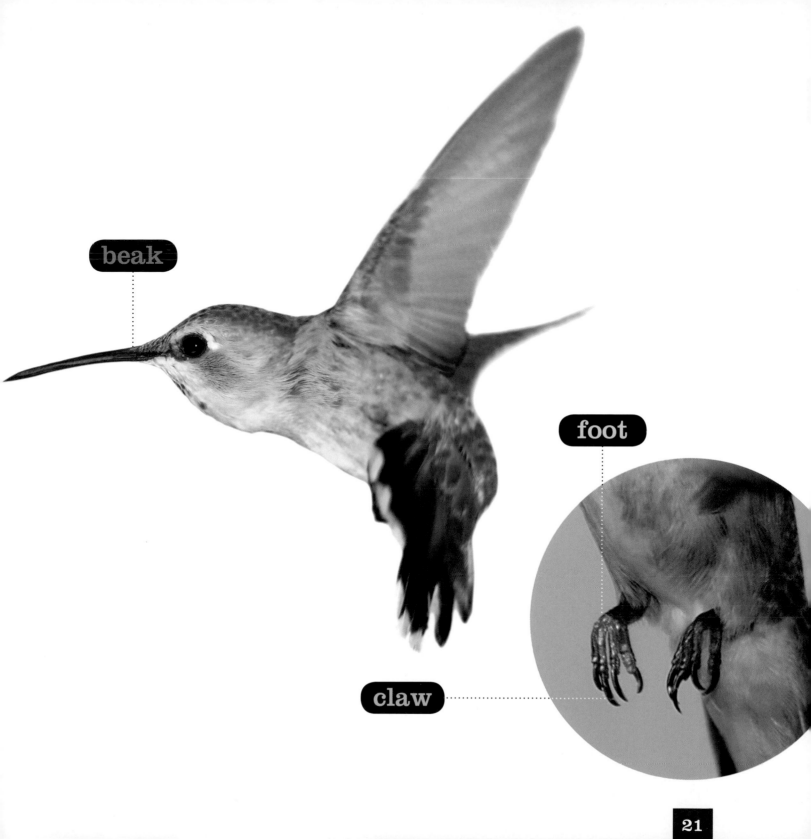

beak

foot

claw

21

beaks: parts of birds' faces that stick out

hover: stay in one place in the air

nectar: a sweet liquid that flowers make

Read More

Bader, Bonnie. *Hummingbirds.*
New York: Grosset & Dunlap, 2015.

Borgert-Spaniol, Megan. *Hummingbirds.*
Minneapolis: Bellwether Media, 2014.

Websites

DLTK's Hummingbird Toilet Paper Roll Craft
www.dltk-kids.com/animals/mhummingbird.htm
Make a hummingbird using a cardboard tube.

National Wildlife Federation: Family Fun
http://www.nwf.org/kids/family-fun.aspx
Search for fun hummingbird crafts and activities.

Index